Going to Boarding School

By Caleb Hippisley

Illustrated by Anton Syadrov

I0162911

Library For All Ltd.

Quandamooka was my Country, my home. It had beautiful sandy beaches and crystal-clear waters. Dolphins and turtles played all day.

My Ancestors lived here for thousands of years. I loved getting to see the rich history left behind in Midden Beds and Bora Rings, still full of cultural traditions.

My name is Caleb, and I lived on my Country. I lived with my parents and brothers in a beach shack. My parents hoped to one day build a big home that would fit all our mob during family gatherings.

I loved playing football and I always have a football in my hand. I loved playing with my siblings on the beach. My favourite team was the Rabbitohs!

If I was really lucky, sometimes my dad would take me to the big game in the city.

I loved sports and I was a good fullback in my team, the Redland Parrots. I dreamed of being a famous footballer and playing with the Rabbitohs.

But my parents wanted me to have a good education and opportunities that they didn't have.

They helped me get a scholarship to a school in the big city. I would be the first in my family to move away from our Country and finish high school.

"I'm nervous," I said to Dad. I was going to be living in a boarding school now, away from all my family. It was scary!

Dad knelt in front of me. "You will do us proud, my son," he said, smiling. "This is a big opportunity to go to a good school and get a good career. This is something your mother and I never had. It's different for you mob now. You need to embrace these opportunities and make the most of them, Caleb."

I was scared and afraid of leaving everything I knew behind. I loved being on my Country and feeling at peace.

But I packed my bags and set off — not forgetting my football!

The boarding house was big, loud, and scary. I didn't like it. I found it difficult to make friends when I felt like this.

I missed my family and my friends! I didn't want to meet new people, I just wanted to go home.

But then, I found out there were brother boys just like me at boarding school. They were also from remote communities around Australia, and they understood what it's like to miss Country.

They also loved football, and the Rabbitohs!

I was starting to make new friends, and that helped me miss home a little less.

Things were different at boarding school, they had so many rules. We had to be in bed by a certain time and we had dinner all together in a huge dining hall.

It was different.

But sometimes at night, we were allowed to play football together.

My new friends and I spent hours playing football, acting like we were sports stars and pretending like we'd just won the grand final.

It was amazing having friends who were so much like me, but also different.

I still missed home sometimes, though, and it was hard.

Some weekends and holidays we were allowed to go home, and my parents let my friends come over. I was proud to show off my Country and play footy together on the beach and field.

I learned that home is where the heart is.

When I finish high school, my family will be so proud of me, and my future will be bright. I can be whatever I want to be.

Watch out world, here I come!

You can use these questions to talk about this book with your family, friends and teachers.

What did you learn from this book?

Describe this book in one word. Funny? Scary? Colourful? Interesting?

How did this book make you feel when you finished reading it?

What was your favourite part of this book?

Download the Library For All Reader app from libraryforall.org

About the author

Caleb Hippisley is from Quandamooka Country. His clan group is Pitta Pitta in Queensland, and his mob is Boulia. He loves watching football with his family and going fishing out on their boat.

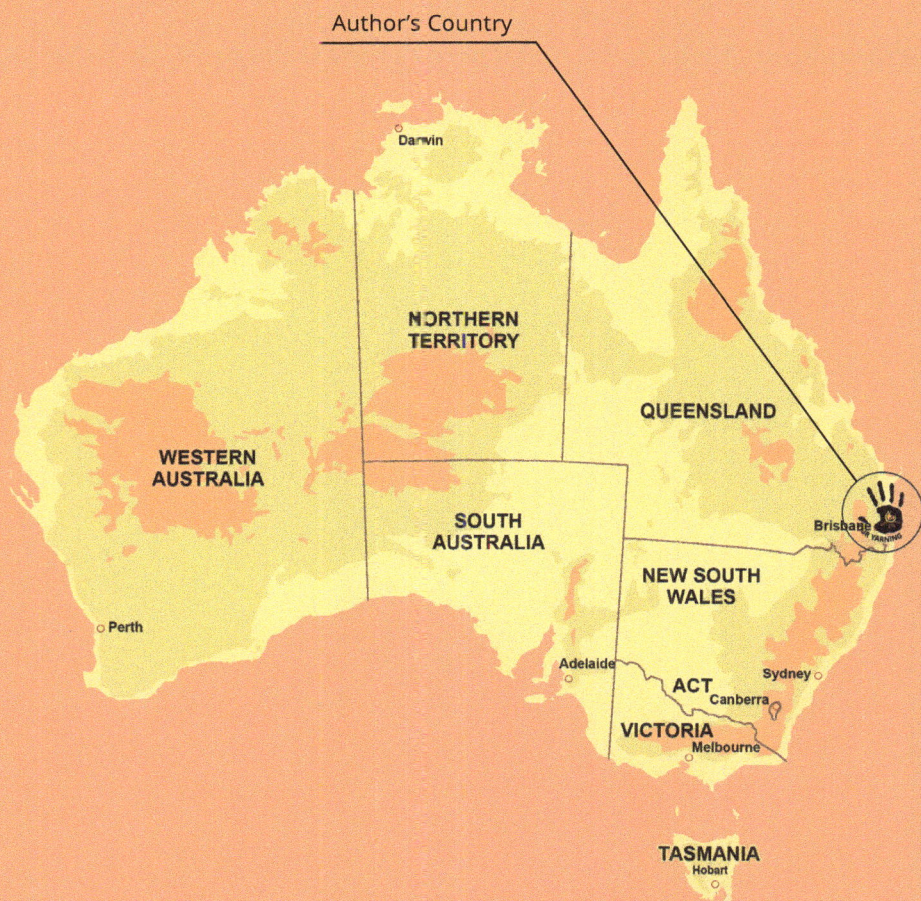

Author's Country

NORTHERN TERRITORY

Darwin

QUEENSLAND

WESTERN AUSTRALIA

SOUTH AUSTRALIA

NEW SOUTH WALES

Brisbane

Perth

Adelaide

Sydney

ACT
Canberra

VICTORIA
Melbourne

TASMANIA
Hobart

Our Yarning

The Our Yarning collection aligns with the Australian Curriculum through the Cross-Curriculum Priorities — Aboriginal and Torres Strait Islander Histories and Cultures. The collection provides an authentic opportunity for learning and embedding Aboriginal and Torres Strait Islander perspectives because it is written by Aboriginal and Torres Strait Islander people.

We know that children learn better, and enjoy reading more, when they see themselves in the stories, characters and illustrations of the books they read.

To download the app, visit the Google Play Store or Apple Store and search 'Our Yarning'.

libraryforall.org

You're reading Middle Primary

Learner – Beginner readers

Start your reading journey with short words,
big ideas and plenty of pictures.

Level 1 – Rising readers

Raise your reading level with more words,
simple sentences and exciting images.

Level 2 – Eager readers

Enjoy your reading time with familiar words,
but complex sentences.

Level 3 – Progressing readers

Develop your reading skills with creative stories
and some challenging vocabulary.

Level 4 – Fluent readers

Step up your reading skills with playful narratives,
new words and fun facts.

Middle Primary – Curious readers

Discover your world through science and stories.

Upper Primary – Adventurous readers

Explore your world through science and stories.

Library For All is an Australian not for profit organisation with a mission to make knowledge accessible to all via an innovative digital library solution. Visit us at libraryforall.org

Going to Boarding School

First published 2024

Published by Library For All Ltd
Email: info@libraryforall.org
URL: libraryforall.org

This book was created in collaboration with Yalari to improve and support the educational outcomes of First Nations children in Australia. We thank Yalari for their ongoing support of the Our Yarning program.

Educating Indigenous Children

Our Yarning logo design by Jason Lee, Bidjipidji Art

Original illustrations by Anton Syadrov

Going to Boarding School
Hippisley, Caleb
ISBN: 978-1-923207-54-7
SKU04421